NATURE DETECTIVE

British Trees

Victoria Munson

WAYLAND

First published in 2015 by Wayland
Copyright © Wayland 2015

Wayland
338 Euston Road
London NW1 3BH

Wayland Australia
Level 17/207 Kent Street
Sydney, NSW 2000

Designer: Elaine Wilkinson
Consultant: Max Coleman, Royal Botanic
Gardens Edinburgh

Acknowledgements:
Corbis: 38 Francesc Muntada; 48 Eric Crichton;
FLPA: 15, 23, Marcus Webb; 16 Joan Hutchings;
23 Marcus Webb; 42 David Hosking; Getty: 12
GettyDEA/RANDOM; 50 DEA/S. MONTANARI/
Getty; 55 John Lawson, Belhaven; Istock:15
inset Matauw; 32 RelaxFoto.de; 37 abzee; 41
mtreasure; 47 amete; 53 Empato; Shutterstock: 4
top Dmitry Naumov; 4 bottom Maryna Pleshkun;
5 Kevin Eaves; 6 centre jopelka; 6 bottom left
Martin Fowler; 6 bottom right TV; 7 left HHelene;
7 bottom right Kazakov Maksim; 8 middle BMJ;
8 bottom right Quanthem; 8 bottom left Buquet
Christophe; 9 top Smit; 9 bottom Sally Wallis;
10 Catalin Petolea; 11 Martin Fowler; 11 inset
Brzostowska;12 inset Birgit Brandlhuber; 13
Bildagentur Zoonar GmbH;14 Ralf Neumann; 17
Bildagentur Zoonar GmbH; 18 inset HHelene;
18 ZanozaRu;19 Maxal Tamor; 19 inset Vitalii
Hulai; 20 Louis W; 20 inset Mageon; 21 Ralf
Neumann; 21 inset dabjola; 22 Semmick Photo;
22 inset defotoberg; 23 inset Richard Peterson;
24 Symbiot; 24 inset top anmo; 24 inset bottom
Yu Lan; 25 filmfoto; 25 inset Scisetti Alfio; 26
Martin Fowler; 27 Imcsike; 28 LensTravel; 29
Daniel Prude; 30 Gl0ck; 31 Digoarpi; 33 Dainis
Derics; 33 inset Tamara Kulikova; 34 Volker
Rauch; 34 inset Ziablik; 35 Erni; 35 inset dabjola;
36 Bildagentur Zoonar GmbH; 36 inset jopelka;
37 inset left Brzostowska; 37 top right majaan;
38 inset AlasdairJames; 39 Kamzara; 40 EMJAY
SMITH; 40 inset Lumir Jurka Lumis; 41 inset
berries Mageon; 43 istockGucio_55; 43 inset
Andrea Wilhelm; 44 Robert Biedermann; 45 inset
Mageon; 45 Ivan Protsiuk; 46 jps; 46 inset duvduv;
48 inset jiangdi; 49 Andy Roland; 49 inset Martin
Fowler; 50 inset svetico; 51 Zyankarlo; 51 inset
Bronwyn Photo; 52 dinkaspell; 52 inset Tulakh; 54
inset kkubicka; 54 ischte; 55 inset M. Cornelius;
56 diak; 56 inset Martin Fowler; 57 Margrit Hirsch;
58 bottom Dmitry Naumov; Peter Bull: 59. With
thanks, for their inspiration and advice, to Alan and
Ann Brooker, and Lily and Polly Munson.

A cataloguing record for this title is available at the
British Library.
Dewey number: 582.1'6'0941-dc23
ISBN: 978 0 7502 9208 5
Ebook ISBN: 978 07502 9324 2

Printed in China

Wayland, part of Hachette Children's Group and
published by Hodder and Stoughton Limited.
www.hachette.co.uk

Contents

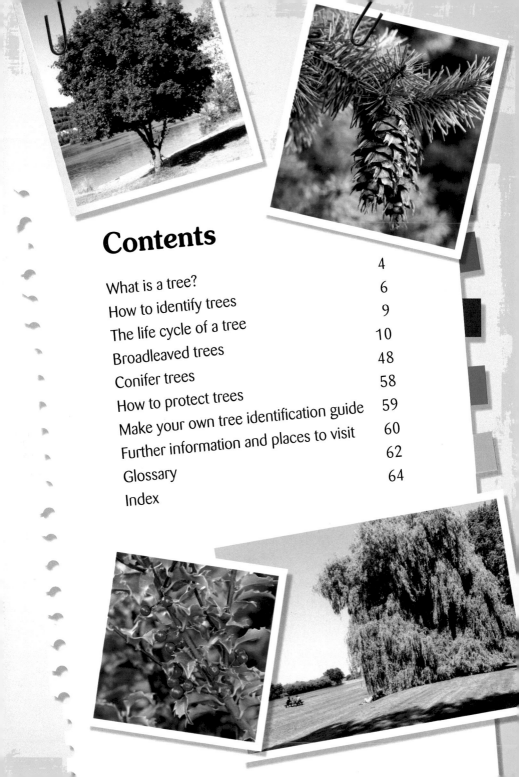

What is a tree?

A tree is a plant with a large woody stem called its trunk, from which grows many branches and leaves. Shrubs are similar to trees, but they don't grow as large and have several stems rather than one trunk.

Types of tree

Trees are divided into three groups: broadleaved trees, conifer trees and palm trees. In Britain, we have mainly broadleaved and conifer trees. Palm trees usually grow in warmer places in the world. Broadleaved trees have flat leaves and their seeds are in fruits, such as nuts and berries. Conifers have needle-like or scaly leaves. Their fruits are called cones.

Broadleaved trees
in autumn

Seasons

Most broadleaved trees are deciduous, which means they lose their leaves in autumn. Their leaves change colour at this time. New green leaves grow in the spring. Conifer trees are mostly evergreen. Evergreen trees also shed their leaves, but a little at a time. These trees never look bare and always have a covering of leaves whatever the season.

Conifer trees
in winter

Different types of tree together in a park.

Species

There are about 250 species of tree native to Europe. However, many more species have been introduced, brought to this country, from other countries. Some of these introduced trees can be found in parks and gardens, others are in plantations. This book describes 48 of the most commonly found species, native or introduced, that can be found in Britain.

Scientific names

Each species of tree has its own unique scientific name. This name is the same around the world. Trees also have a common name, such as Oak or Horse Chestnut. The common name might be different in each country, or even within the same country. In Britain, for example, Rowan is also known as Mountain Ash.

There may be more than 60,000 species of tree growing worldwide.

How to identify trees

There are many features you can note down to help you identify trees, such as leaf shape, seeds, fruit, flowers, buds and bark. You could take this book out with you to help you identify trees. Never break off parts of a tree to bring home as this could damage the tree.

Leaves

A good starting point is to look at the shape of leaves. Are they lobed, needle-like, toothed or heart-shaped? How are the leaves arranged? Look to see if they are opposite, alternate or spiral.

Lobed
(English Oak)

Needle-like
(Scots Pine)

Heart-shaped
(Silver Birch)

Rounded (Aspen)

Toothed (Common Lime)

Branches and bark

Twigs and branches make up the crown of a tree. The crown is the top shape of a tree. It can be spreading like an Oak or conical-shaped like a Norway Spruce. A crown can also change shape as a tree gets older.

Bark provides a protective layer for the trunk. The bark splits as the tree grows, cracking and peeling away to be continually replaced by new bark. The patterns and colour of bark can help you identify the tree.

Buds

In late winter and early spring, buds can be found on the trees. Some trees, such as the Horse Chestnut, have large sticky buds. Birch trees have small pointed buds.

Flowers

In spring, you can see many types of catkins and flowers. Some catkins are short and fat like the Alder, or thin and hairy like the Aspen. Flowers grow on their own, or in groups as clusters or spikes. Horse Chestnuts have large, upright white-pink flowers on spikes. Rowans have clusters of small white flowers.

Wild Pear flowers

Crab apple flowers

Fruits and seeds

In late summer and autumn, you can identify a tree by its fruit. There are edible fruits such as apples and elderberries, or nuts and seeds such as acorns and walnuts that animals like to eat.

Elder berries

Sweet chestnuts

Seasons

The time of year it is will also help you to identify trees. If it is autumn or winter and the tree still has its leaves, then this means the tree must be an evergreen, such as Holly or Scots Pine. If the tree has shed its leaves, then it is a deciduous broadleaved tree, such as the English Oak. In winter, it is easier to see the colour of the bark and the shape of the branches. In spring, there are lots of buds and flowers to help with identification. In summer and autumn, there are fruits and seeds to find.

The life cycle of a tree

In spring, insects, or the wind, carry pollen from flower to flower. Seeds form from the female parts of flowers and then fall from the tree and are spread by the wind, or by birds and animals. Some seeds have wings, such as Sycamore or Ash, to help them glide from the tree. Seeds that are in berries attract animals to eat them. The seed is carried in the animal until it is excreted later. Some nuts, such as acorns and hazelnuts, are collected and buried by animals, who may forget about them so the nuts remain buried and then start to grow.

Once a seed is in the ground, it grows roots and sprouts leaves. It grows bigger and bigger. A young tree is called a tiny sapling and this will take many years to become a fully grown tree. Once the tree is a few years' old then it can produce seeds.

Many saplings are eaten by animals.

English Oak

Scientific name: *Quercus robur*
Height: over 20 metres
Life span: up to 800 years

Most recognised by its acorn fruits, the English Oak is common across Britain. The acorns sit in scaly cups at the end of long stalks. Leaves have four to seven wavy-edged lobes. The tree has a broad, uneven crown and the grey bark has deep ridges and cracks.

Acorns are not produced until a tree is at least 40 years old.

Sessile Oak

Scientific name: *Quercus petraea*
Height: up to 40 metres
Life span: up to 1,000 years

One Oak tree can produce up to 50,000 acorns in one year.

Common in north and west Britain, Sessile Oaks have straighter branches and a more upright trunk than an English Oak. The leaves do not have rounded lobes but are more pointed and on longer stalks. In autumn, acorns are on almost stalkless twigs.

Turkey oak

Scientific name: *Quercus cerris*
Height: up to 30 metres
Life span: up to 800 years

A Turkey Oak looks very similar to the Sessile and English Oak, but its acorn cups are hairy. The acorns are an orange colour at the base to a greeny-brown tip. Leaves are lobed and rough and thick to touch.

Oak wood is very strong and has been used for thousands of years for ship building and for house beams.

12

White Willow

Scientific name: *Salix alba*
Height: up to 25 metres
Life span: up to 200 years

White Willow leaves are thin and oval-shaped. They have a fine covering of white hairs on the underside, giving the tree its name. Willows grow well in wet ground so are often found near rivers and streams.

Weeping Willow

Scientific name: *Salix x sepulcralis*
Height: up to 12 metres
Life span: up to 100 years

The Weeping Willow is a cross between the White Willow and the Chinese Weeping Willow. It is a large tree often found near ponds and rivers where its leaves and shoots hang, or weep, into the water. The leaves are long and narrow. Catkins are 3–4 cm long and appear in spring at the same time as the leaves.

Goat Willow

Scientific name: *Salix caprea*
Height: up to 12 metres
Life span: 150–300 years

The Goat Willow is also called the 'Pussy Willow' because its silky, grey female flowers look like cats' paws. It is a small tree mostly found near rivers and wet areas. It is easy to tell apart from other Willows because its oval leaves are broader than the leaves on other types of Willow tree.

Crack Willow

Scientific name: *Salix fragilis*
Height: up to 25 metres
Life span: up to 100 years

Crack Willow is one of Britain's largest native willow trees. It is sometimes mistaken for the White Willow, but the Crack Willow's leaves are shorter and do not have white hairs underneath. Yellow male catkins and green female catkins grow on separate trees. Once pollinated, the female catkins turn into white, woolly seeds.

Common Osier

Scientific name: *Salix viminalis*
Height: up to 7 metres
Life span: up to 70 years

Osier is often found in wet habitats next to rivers and streams. It has glossy green leaves, which are very long and thin. It is fast-growing and its shoots have been used for many hundreds of years to make baskets.

Aspen

Scientific name:
Populus tremula
Height: up to 20 metres
Life span: up to 100 years

Aspen is more often found in the
north of Britain than the south. Its trunk
and branches are thin. The rounded leaves have
small teeth on the edge. Leaf stalks are unusually long
and flattened. In spring, the Aspen's buds are pointed.
The catkins are long and green with white fluff.

Black Poplar

Scientific name:
Populus nigra
Height: up to 30 metres
Life span: up to 200 years

The Black Poplar is now the most endangered native tree in Britain. It grows in very wet ground such as flood plains and has become endangered because it often gets diseases. Its name comes from its dark-brown bark that looks black. It is a tall, thin tree with shiny, green, heart-shaped leaves. You can tell it apart from other Poplars because it has lumps and bumps on its trunk.

White Poplar

Scientific name: *Populus alba*
Height: up to 20 metres
Life span: up to 50 years

catkins

The White Poplar gets its name because, from a distance, when the tree is young, it looks white. The leaves have five toothed lobes with white hairs on the underside. Its bark is a light-grey colour.

Silver Birch

Scientific name: *Betula pendula*
Height: up to 30 metres
Life span: 80–150 years

— catkins

Silver Birch gets its name from its silver-coloured trunk. The bark peels off in strips leaving dark marks. The leaves are heart-shaped with toothed edges. Male catkins droop downwards and are about 3 cm long. Female catkins are smaller and are upright.

Common Alder

Scientific name: *Alnus glutinosa*
Height: up to 20 metres
Life span: around 100 years

The seeds from an Alder will float on the surface of a river until they land on a bank and start to grow.

Alder grows best in damp areas such as wet woodland and riverbanks. The leaves are rounded with toothed edges and noticeable veins. Its bark is dark grey. In spring, male catkins are a dark yellow-brown and about 2–6 cm long. Female flowers are smaller, cone-shaped and turn from red to green.

Common Hazel

Hazel nuts

Scientific name: *Corylus avellana*
Height: up to 6 metres
Life span: around 100 years

Hazel leaves are round with a pointed tip and a toothed edge.
Yellow male catkins are known as 'lambs' tails'. Female flowers are
small and pink. The tree's nuts are eaten by humans and animals.

Hornbeam

Scientific name: *Carpinus betulus*
Height: up to 30 metres
Life span: up to 300 years

Hornbeam wood is very hard and so has been used for furniture, chopping boards and floorboards.

Hornbeams are large, wide trees that look similar to Beech trees. Leaves are oval and pointed with finely toothed edges and prominent veins, but they are smaller than Beech leaves. The bark is pale grey with upright markings, which becomes more ridged with age.

Beech nuts

Common Beech

Scientific name: *Fagus sylvatica*
Height: up to 40 metres
Life span: 150–200 years

Beech trees are tall with a spreading dome-shaped crown and smooth grey bark. The leaves are pointed, toothed ovals with 5–9 veins. In spring, they have long, pointed, copper-coloured buds. Yellowy-green flowers become a green spiky husk in which sit shiny, brown beech nuts.

A Beech tree's roots don't grow very deep so they are often one of the first trees to fall in a storm.

Common Ash

Scientific name: *Fraxinus excelsior*
Height: up to 40–45 metres
Life span: up to 400 years

Ash trees don't produce flowers and seeds until they are at least 30-years-old.

These large trees are one of the first to lose their leaves in the autumn. Each leaf is made up of paired-leaflets with one at the end. The leaflets are pointed and toothed. Buds are black and velvety. Its bark is silvery grey. Flowers cluster at the tips of twigs before they turn into ash keys.

Elder

Scientific name: *Sambucus nigra*
Height: up to 15 metres
Life span: up to 60 years

The Elder is a small tree with light-brown bark covered in small bumps. The leaf is made up of 5–7 toothed leaflets. In June and July, the tree is covered in sweet-smelling, white flowers. By August and September, these have turned into purple-black berries (see page 8) that can be made into jam, wine or cordials.

Holly

Scientific name: *Ilex aquifolium*
Height: up to 25 metres
Life span: up to 300 years

Holly berries are poisonous for humans.

Evergreen Holly trees have
tough, spiky leaves. The spikes
are to stop animals from eating them.
Its bark is silver-grey. In spring, Holly has
small, four-petalled, white flowers. Bright red
berries in autumn attract many birds.

Common Lime

Scientific name: *Tilia x europaea*
Height: up to 40 metres
Life span: up to 400 years

The Common Lime has broad, heart-shaped leaves with toothed edges. You can usually find small tufts of creamy white hair in the leaf veins. Limes attract greenfly and blackfly that feed on the leaves making them sticky. Sweet-smelling, yellow-white flowers appear in July and turn into small seed balls. Suckers grow from the base of the tree.

Small Leaved Lime

Scientific name: *Tilia cordata*
Height: up to 30 metres
Life span: over 500 years

Lime flowers are used for herbal tea.

Small Leaved Limes are often planted in residential areas, or in long avenues of country parks, because of their sweet-smelling flowers. The flowers are white-yellow and hang in clusters on a long stalk. Fruits are oval with pointed tips. The hairless leaves are heart-shaped, with a pointed tip at the end.

Large Leaved Lime

Scientific name: *Tilia platyphyllos*
Height: up to 35 metres
Life span: over 1,000 years

This tall tree has, as its name suggests, larger leaves than the Small Leaved Lime. The leaves have a hairy stalk and the bark is dark brown. Fruits are rounded and smooth with pointed tips. This Lime doesn't produce suckers from the base of the tree.

London Plane

Scientific name: *Platanus x hispanica*
Height: up to 35 metres
Life span: up to 500 years

seed balls

Most often found in towns and cities, the London Plane tree is said to make up half of the trees in London. It has large glossy leaves about 10 cm wide, with noticeable veins. As the trunk grows, its grey bark continually flakes off revealing a creamy yellow and light brown bark beneath. Through winter, you can see dried brown seed balls hanging from the branches. Seeds are released from these in spring.

Rowan

Scientific name: *Sorbus aucuparia*
Height: up to 10 metres
Life span: up to 200 years

The Rowan tree is also known as a Mountain Ash because it grows higher up on hills and mountains than most other trees. Toothed leaflets are arranged opposite each other with one leaflet at the end. Creamy white scented flowers grow in tight clusters. The flowers become bright red berries in August and September.

Horse Chestnut

Scientific name: *Aesculus hippocastanum*
Height: up to 40 metres
Life span: up to 300 years

In winter, look out for large, brown-red sticky buds.

These large trees are better-known as 'conker trees'. In summer, Horse Chestnuts are covered in large spikes of white, or pale pink, flowers. The spiny fruits that grow in autumn contain seeds called conkers. Each leaf is made up of 5–7 long leaflets. The greyish-green bark has large flakes breaking from it. Horse Chestnuts are not edible.

Sweet Chestnut

Scientific name: *Castanea sativa*
Height: about 30 metres
Life span: up to 700 years

Sweet Chestnut trees have large oval-shaped, toothed leaves with a pointed tip. Leaves on an older tree can be as long as 20 cm. Male catkins are yellow and hairy, like golden caterpillars. In June or July, female flowers look like green rosettes. In autumn, these form a very prickly case around the seeds.

Roasted Sweet Chestnuts are delicious to eat.

Field Maple

Scientific name: *Acer campestre*
Height: up to 20 metres
Life span: up to 350 years

Field Maple sap can be used to make maple syrup.

This small tree has leaves
with five wavy lobes on long stalks.
In spring, the yellow-green cup-shaped flowers
hang in clusters. These turn into winged fruits.

Sycamore

Scientific name: *Acer pseudoplatanus*
Height: up to 35 metres
Life span: up to 500 years

Sycamore seeds are often called 'helicopters'.

Sycamore leaves have five large lobes with rounded teeth. Small green flowers appear at the same time as the leaves. The flowers form winged seeds that help them to glide far from the tree. The bark is smooth and pinkish-grey, but it begins to flake as the tree gets older.

Wych Elm

Scientific name: *Ulmus glabra*
Height: up to 30 metres
Life span: up to 200 years

Wych Elm has large toothed leaves with a point at the top. The twigs are dark grey and covered in hairs. In spring, purple-black flowers appear before the leaves. The flowers turn into small, flat, papery fruits called 'samaras'. Elm wood is strong and waterproof and so it is often used to make boats, floorboards and furniture.

English Elm

Scientific name: *Ulmus procera*
Height: up to 30 metres
Life span: more than 100 years

English Elms are not very common in Britain anymore because many trees were killed by Dutch Elm disease, which came to Britain in the 1960s. These trees are very hard to tell apart from Wych Elms. English Elms have oval, pointed and hairy buds. Flowers are dark pink.

Whitebeam

Scientific name: *Sorbus aria*
Height: up to 15 metres
Life span: up to 80 years

Whitebeam is also known as
'chess apple', 'quickbeam' and 'white
hazel'. It is a small tree with oval leaves that have a
toothed edge. In spring, the underside of the leaves look
white because they are covered with hairs that then fall off.
The bark is smooth and grey. Clusters of creamy white-coloured
scented flowers turn into green, then red, berry-like fruits.

Hawthorn

Scientific name: *Crataegus monogyna*
Height: 5–12 metres
Life span: up to 250 years

Hawthorn is also called the 'May tree' because it is in full flower throughout May.

Hawthorn can grow as a shrub, hedge or small tree. The stems of a young hawthorn are covered in sharp thorns. The bark is brown and often covered in green algae. Its leaves are small and deeply-lobed. White flowers appear in spring. In autumn, the flowers turn into dark red berries called 'haws'. These can be used in jams and jellies.

Crab Apple

Scientific name: *Malus sylvestris*
Height: up to 10 metres
Life span: up to 100 years

The Crab Apple is a small tree
found mostly in hedgerows or on the
edges of woods. In spring, the tree is covered in
small pink blossom. Its fruits look like apples, but they
only grow to 3 cm. These can be eaten but taste very sour,
so they are mostly used for making jam or wine.

Blackthorn

Scientific name: *Prunus spinosa*
Height: up to 7 metres
Life span: up to 100 years

Blackthorn flowers are edible and the leaves can be made into tea.

Blackthorn, as its name suggests, has thorns on its branches. It is a small tree and is often grown as a hedge. White flowers appear in early spring and, once pollinated, these turn into blue-black fruits called sloes. Slightly wrinkled leaves are oval-shaped, toothed with a point at the tip.

Wild Cherry

Scientific name: *Prunus avium*
Height: up to 30 metres
Life span: up to 60 years

In spring, Wild Cherry is covered in clusters of white blossom.
After pollination, the flowers turn into dark-red cherries. The cherries
can be eaten, but they taste really sour. They are mainly eaten by birds
and small mammals. The shiny bark is deep reddish-brown and the
leaves are oval and toothed with pointed tips.

berries

Bird Cherry

Scientific name: *Prunus padus*
Height: up to 25 metres
Life span: up to 60 years

Found in wet woodland or near streams and rivers, Bird Cherry has greyish-brown bark with dark brown twigs. The leaves are oval with sharply toothed edges and pointed tips. White flowers with toothed petals open in May, on spikes holding 10–40 flowers. The flowers smell of almond. These change into reddish-black, very bitter-tasting, cherries.

Wild Pear

Scientific name: *Pyrus pyraster*
Height: up to 20 metres
Life span: up to 150 years

A Wild Pear's fruit is woody and hard, so people rarely eat it. The leaves are oval with finely-toothed edges. In spring, white flowers cover the tree in clusters. The bark is rough and a grey-brown colour.

Ancient Romans introduced Walnut trees to Britain because they loved walnuts.

Walnut

Scientific name: *Juglans regia*
Height: up to 35 metres
Life span: up to 200 years

Walnut trees are often found in parks and large gardens. They have a broad crown. The 5–9 leaflets are shiny. Male catkins are 5–10 cm long and the pollinated female flowers develop into a green, fleshy fruit that contains a walnut.

Leyland Cypress

Scientific name: X *Cupressocyparis leylandii*
Height: up to 40 metres
Life span: up to 80 years

These tall trees are
often used to make thick hedges.
The bark is red-grey and twigs are thin
and flexible. Leaves are scaly and overlapping
on long twigs. The small ball-shaped cones are brown.

Yew

Scientific name: *Taxus baccata*
Height: up to 30 metres
Life span: over 1,000 years

Yew trees are often found in graveyards. They have a distinctive red flaky bark. The leaves are needle-like, long and narrow. In spring, seeds sit in a bright-red, fleshy cup.

Yew leaves and berries are extremely poisonous to humans.

Common Juniper

Scientific name: *Juniperus communis*
Height: up to 10 metres
Life span: up to 200 years

When crushed, Common Juniper leaves smell of apples or lemons.

Common Juniper is an endangered tree most often found in rocky areas. It is a small tree with needle-like leaves. Male flowers are small and yellow. Green female flowers, once pollinated by the wind, turn into purple, berry-like cones.

Norway Spruce

Scientific name: *Picea abies*
Height: up to 40 metres
Life span: up to 200 years

Some Norway Spruce can live up to 1,000 years.

More familiar as a Christmas tree, the Norway Spruce is a tall, straight tree with a pointed crown. The needle-like leaves are pointed. Female flowers are upright red ovals that, once pollinated, turn into cones with diamond-shaped scales.

51

Larch

Scientific name: *Larix decidua*
Height: up to 30 metres
Life span: up to 250 years

Larch has a cone-shaped crown when young, which becomes broader with age. Light-green needles grow in clumps of 3–40. These turn yellow in the autumn. The bark is a pale, pinky-brown colour. Red-pink female flowers turn into egg-shaped cones. Male cones are yellowish. Both take a year to turn fully brown.

Larch timber is used for gates, fences and garden furniture.

Douglas Fir

Scientific name: *Pseudotsuga menziesii*
Height: up to 55 metres
Life span: more than 1,000 years

Douglas Firs were brought to Britain from North America in 1827 by the Scottish botanist, David Douglas. They are now one of the tallest trees found in Britain. The pointed, green needles are soft and have a white band underneath. Long cones hang down from the branches.

Scots Pine

Scientific name: *Pinus sylvestris*
Height: up to 35 metres
Life span: up to 700 years

The wood from Scots Pine trees is used to make telegraph poles.

Scots Pine is found most commonly in the Scottish Highlands, but can also be found in parks and gardens across Britain. You can easily identify a Scots Pine because the lower part of the trunk is grey, while the upper part is rust-red. No other pine tree is like this. The leaves are needles about 5 cm long, which grow in pairs along a stem.

Sitka Spruce

Scientific name: *Picea sitchensis*
Height: up to 60 metres
Life span: over 700 years

All spruces have a woody peg at the base of every needle.

Sitka Spruces are most commonly found growing in plantations, where they are harvested for their timber and pulped to make paper. They have a straight, conical-shaped trunk and a pointed crown. The bark is purple-grey. Female flowers grow right at the top of the tree and are red, upright and oval. These change to pale green cones that ripen to creamy-brown in autumn.

Cedar of Lebanon

Scientific name: *Cedrus libani*
Height: up to 35 metres
Life span: up to 350 years

Cedars are tall trees with
a broad crown. They are often found
in the parks and gardens of stately homes.
Leaves are needle-shaped and arranged in spirals.
Cedar cones point upwards and are smooth and
egg-shaped. They are produced once every two years.

Monkey Puzzle

Scientific name: *Araucaria araucana*
Height: up to 50 metres
Life span: up to 150 years

This unusual tree is usually only found in gardens and stately homes. It was brought to Britain by the botanist Archibald Menzies in 1795. Monkey Puzzle trees have green, glossy, sharply-pointed leaves that overlap and completely cover each branch. The tree gets its common name because people thought its spiny branches would puzzle a climbing monkey.

Protecting trees

Trees are essential to our planet. They make oxygen that we breathe, and take in pollution from the air. They are home for thousands of different types of wildlife. Some of the fruits and nuts that we eat come from trees. We use trees to make lots of things, such as furniture, buildings and boats. Around the world, too many trees are being cut down. We need to make sure that there are enough trees in the future.

You can help!

Trees are cut down to make paper. You can help to protect trees by recycling paper. Always use both sides of a piece of paper. Use scraps of paper for making lists or drawing sketches.

Recycle it!

When you've finished with the paper, make sure it goes into a recycling box. Ask your parents to buy recycled paper, kitchen rolls and toilet paper. Check with your school to see if they use recycled paper, too.

Make your own tree identification guide

You will need:
- leaves
- kitchen roll paper
- heavy books
- a notebook
- a pen
- glue.

1 Collect different shaped and different sized leaves that have fallen from a tree.

2 Lay them flat between two sheets of kitchen roll paper and place them in the middle of a heavy book.

3 After one month, your leaves will be really flat. Take them out and glue them into your notebook.

4 Use this book, and other books, to identify the leaf. Write down the name of the tree next to the leaf and and some other details about the tree, such as when you saw it, the colour of its bark or if there were any seeds.

Sycamore leaf.
14 July.

Smooth, grey bark

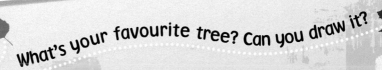

What's your favourite tree? Can you draw it?

Further information

Places to visit

Royal Botanic Gardens at Kew
Richmond
Surrey TW9 3AB
www.rbgkew.org.uk

Royal Botanic Garden Edinburgh
Inverleith Row
Edinburgh EH3 5LR
www.rbge.org.uk

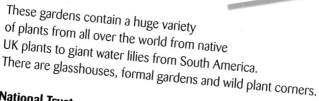

These gardens contain a huge variety of plants from all over the world from native UK plants to giant water lilies from South America. There are glasshouses, formal gardens and wild plant corners.

National Trust
The National Trust takes care of forests, woods, fens, beaches, farmland, moorland and nature reserves as well as historic houses and gardens. Find a new place to visit.
www.nationaltrust.org.uk/visit/places/find-a-place-to-visit

Useful books

I Love This Tree by Anna Claybourne (Watts, 2015)

Nature in Your Neighbourhood: Trees and Flowers by Clare Collinson (Watts, 2015)

Useful websites

www.woodlands.co.uk/blog/tree-identification/
An excellent online tree identification website. On it's home page, you can also buy a piece of woodland.

The Woodland Trust
www.woodlandtrust.org.uk/learn/british-trees/
Identification guides to native and non-native British trees, including sections on places to visit, threats to woodland and how to record trees and nature.

www.naturedetectives.co.uk
Visit the Nature Detective's activity pages, part of The Woodland Trust's website, for fun ideas, activity sheets and events. It also includes resources for schools.

Royal Forestry Society
www.rfs.org.uk/learning
This site has a useful A-Z of trees giving information about characteristics, distribution and human and wildlife value.

Natural History Museum
www.nhm.ac.uk/nature-online/british-natural-history/urban-tree-survey/identify-trees/tree-factsheets/index.html
The Natural History Museum's fact sheets provide information about many different species of tree.

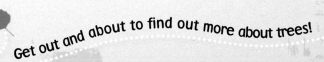

Get out and about to find out more about trees!

Glossary

bark the outside of a tree's trunk

broadleaved broadleaved trees have flat leaves and their seeds are in fruits, such as nuts and berries

catkins petalless flowers that hang from trees and are usually pollinated by the wind

conifer conifer trees have needle-like or scaly leaves. Their fruits are cones.

crown the top part of a tree

deciduous a tree that sheds its leaves in autumn

edible can be eaten

endangered a plant or animal that is very rare and in danger of becoming extinct

evergreen a tree that has leaves on it all year round

excreted passed through the body as waste matter

floodplain an area of low-growing ground next to a river

habitat a place where a plant or an animal lives in the wild

introduced a tree that has been brought to a country where it doesn't usually grow

keys seeds with a wing

leaflet a small separate part of a leaf

life span the length of time that an organism usually lives for.

lobe the rounded edge of a leaf

native a tree or plant that grows naturally in an area

nut a fruit that consists of a hard shell surrounding the seed

plantations areas where large numbers of trees are planted to be used for their wood

pollination the spread of pollen from one flower to another

sap a sticky juice inside a tree

species one of the groups into which trees, plants and other living things are divided

suckers a new branch that grows from the base of a tree

Index

9780750283410

9780750292764

9780750292849

9780750283427

9780750292856

9780750292085

 Let's investigate!